ALSO BY VERA PAVLOVA

Iz vos'mi knig (From Eight Books, 2009)

Na tom beregu rechi (On the Other Shore of Speech, 2009)

Mudraya dura (The Wise Fool, 2008)

Tri knigi (Three Books, 2007)

Pis'ma v sosednuyu komnatu
(Letters to a Room Next Door, 2006)

Ruchnaya klad' (Carry-on Luggage, 2006)

Po obe storony potseluya (On Both Sides of the Kiss, 2004)

Vezdes' (Here and Everywhere, 2002)

Intimnyy dnevnik otlichnicy
(The Intimate Diary of a Straight-A Student, 2001)

Sovershennoletiye (Coming of Age, 2001)

Chetvertyi son (The Fourth Dream, 2000)

Liniya otryva (Tear on This Line, 2000)

Vtoroy yazyk (The Second Tongue, 1998)

Nebesnoye zhivotnoye (The Heavenly Beast, 1997)

If There Is Something to Desire

If There Is Something to Desire

ONE HUNDRED POEMS

Vera Pavlova

Translated from the Russian by Steven Seymour

ALFRED A. KNOPF NEW YORK 2012

THIS IS A BORZOI BOOK
PUBLISHED BY ALFRED A. KNOPF

Published in the United States by Alfred A. Knopf,
a division of Random House, Inc., New York,
and in Canada by Random House of
Canada, Limited, Toronto.
www.aaknopf.com

Knopf, Borzoi Books, and the colophon are registered
trademarks of Random House, Inc.

Library of Congress Cataloguing-in-Publication Data
Pavlova, Vera (Vera Anatol'evna)
[Poems. English. Selections]
If there is something to desire : one hundred poems / by Vera
Pavlova ; translated from the Russian by Steven Seymour.—
1st ed.
p.   cm.
"This is a Borzoi book."
ISBN 978-0-375-71189-3
1. Pavlova, Vera (Vera Anatol'evna)—Translations into
English.   I. Seymour, Steven.   II. Title.
PG3485.A875I37 2010
891.71'5—dc22   2009022095

Manufactured in the United States of America
Published January 21, 2010
First Paperback Edition January 12, 2012

The author and the translator
dedicate this book to
Bill Wadsworth,
with love and gratitude

Contents

CONTENTS

CONTENTS

CONTENTS

CONTENTS

CONTENTS

If There Is Something to Desire

1

In a nook I write,
you would say crochet
a fuzzy mitten
for a child to be born.

My parents were virgins.

At twenty-two, even then it was unusual.

And although Dad was known as a skirt chaser around the
women's dorm,

he visited women in order to get some food,

because he was living on his stipend.

At first he visited Mom also in order to eat.

And when at the school they started talking about a possible
wedding,

someone slipped her a copy of

"How a Girl Becomes a Woman."

Mom threw it out unopened.

It was scary for them to make me.

It was weird for them to make me.

It was painful for them to make me.

It was funny for them to make me.

And I absorbed:

Life is scary.

Life is weird.

Life is painful.

Life is very funny.

3

On his back, on Grandma's bed, my brother was flailing his
      tiny legs.
He's gonna fall, I thought. But he would not.
Why isn't he falling? I wondered. He was flailing his legs.
He's gotta fall! Pulled him by the legs closer to the edge.
Still would not fall. Pulled some more. He was flailing
      his legs.
Pulled a bit more. With a horrific crash he fell head down,
      the dummy,
and bawled so loud that Grandma came running:
Who left the baby unattended? — I said: *Mom did.*
But not out loud, trembling in the dark under Grandma's bed.

4

Fell in love in sleep,
woke up in tears:
never have loved anyone so much,
never has anyone loved me so.
Had no time for even a kiss,
nor to ask his name.
Now I pass
sleepless nights
dreaming of him.

5

Mother left early for work.
Dawn was soiling the sky.
Virginity? The hell with it! High time.
The first night happened at dawn,
on September the first.

The day before I had promised him,
and I keep my word. Lover, take
your reward for the evenings
spent hiding in crannies and nooks.

So this is what "being a wife" means?

6

Learn to look past,
to be the first to part.
Tears, saliva, sperm
are no solvents for solitude.
On gilded wedding bowls,
on the plastic cups of one-night stands,
an eye can see, if skilled,
solitude's bitter residue.

7

If there is something to desire,
there will be something to regret.
If there is something to regret,
there will be something to recall.
If there is something to recall,
there was nothing to regret.
If there was nothing to regret,
there was nothing to desire.

8

A beast in winter,
a plant in spring,
an insect in summer,
a bird in autumn.
The rest of the time I am a woman.

9

I broke your heart.
Now barefoot I tread
on shards.

10

I feel
your flesh so full
in me,
that I do not feel it
at all
on top of me.
Is all of you
within me,
a thing-in-me?
Or is all of you
outside of me,
and only seems to be?

11

Let us touch each other
while we still have hands,
palms, forearms, elbows . . .
Let us love each other for misery,
let us torture each other,
mangle, maim,
to remember better,
to part with less pain.

12

Tenderly on a tender surface
the best of my lines are written:
with the tip of my tongue on your palate,
on your chest in tiny letters,
on your belly . . .
But, darling, I wrote them
pianissimo!
May I erase with my lips
your exclamation mark?

13

What cannot be swallowed,
what does not go down the gullet,
what only stays in the mouth
and is absorbed by the tongue and the palate,
what cannot be called nourishment,
can well be called a wild strawberry,
a first and a last kiss,
a grape, semen, a wafer.

14

No love? Let us make it!
Done. Next? Let us make
care, tenderness, courage,
jealousy, glut, lies.

15

Do you know what you lacked?
That dose of contempt without which
you cannot flip a woman on her back
to make her flounder like a turtle,
to make the heartless fool realize:
she cannot flip back on her own.

16

Whose face and body would I like to have?
The face and body of Nike.
I would fly past all those Venuses,
would have nothing to do with Apollos.
With the wind chilling my shoulder
I would leave behind forever
the hall of plaster copies!

17

Why is the word *yes* so brief?
It should be
the longest,
the hardest,
so that you could not decide in an instant to say it,
so that upon reflection you could stop
in the middle of saying it.

18

—Sing me The Song of Songs.
—Don't know the words.
—Then sing the notes.
—Don't know the notes.
—Then simply hum.
—Forgot the tune.
—Then press my ear
to your ear
and sing what you hear.

19

A girl sleeps as if
she were in someone's dream;
a woman sleeps as if
tomorrow a war will begin;
an old woman sleeps as if
it were enough to feign being dead
and death might pass her by
on the far outskirts of sleep.

20

One Touch in Seven Octaves

I

A light touch with a slant
like a first-grader's handwriting, with a tilt:
you brush away a hair from my cheek
with a motion vaguely tender, stretching
my face slightly upward and to the left,
turning me into a doe-eyed geisha.
With a slant, yet in a straight line:
the shortest and the quickest path.

II

The trick is in the suffixes, diminutive and endearing:
to diminish first, then to caress,
and by caressing to reduce to naught,
and then to search in panic, where can you be?
Have I dropped you into the gap
between the body and the soul?
And all the while you are right here,
in my arms. So heavy, so enormous!

III

First, cursory caresses, on the surface,
light, a kind of coloratura: crumbs of
pizzicato in spots which seemingly require
a brusque, tempestuous treatment,
then with a bow across the secret strings,
the ones that were not touched at the beginning,
then across the non-existent strings or, more exactly,
the ones we have never suspected of existing.

IV

Are my palms rubbing your shoulders,
or are your smooth shoulders rubbing my palms,
making them drier, sharper, more perfect?
The more repetitive a caress, the more healing it is.
Water slowly grinds stone; caresses
make the body light, chiseled, compact,
the way it wants to be,
the way it once had been.

V

Who plays blindman's buff with those aged twenty,
hide-and-seek with those aged thirty?
Love does. Ah, the silky pelts,
the simple rules, the witless stakes!
Is it easy at thirty-five to say good-bye to love?
It is, not for the reasons of great shame involved,
but because there is no spot more tender, rosier,
more concealed than a scar.

VI

Within a hand's reach from the foreskin
is fleshlessness, dense, resonant, boundless.
Touching, because of its nature, takes part
in the mystery of disembodiment.
I am rid of the body, but the shiver stays,
and so do the pain, the joy.
The shiver, the pain, the joy have no fear
that the skin might never reappear.

VII

How tender the sensation of ants racing,
how many shivers in a slow progression!
Some take no less than a full five minutes
to get from one vertebra to the next.
For years a gentle hand has been the trainer
coaxing them to run from one tiny hair
to the next, until the finish line,
until it is madness, until . . . *Hey,
are you sleeping?*

21

The first kiss in the morning
tastes like the first kiss on Earth.
My waking soul is innocent,
as I lie next to the tenant
of my best dreams.
When I caress him, I know:
a kiss is preverbal,
a word is a kiss's junior.

22

Enough painkilling, heal.
Enough cajoling, command,
even if your fiery joys
mean endless inequality
and melt our vessels
that are dispensable.
Enough rehashing, create.
Enough lying to the sick:
they will not get well.

23

Mom was an axiom.
Dad was a theorem.
I was a sleeping beauty
in the cradle of home.
The cradle has capsized.
Now the end is the means.
Cradlewrecked beauty, keep an eye
on your mother who is an infant again.

24

Why do I recite my poems by heart?
Because I write them by heart,
because I know that kind of spleen
by heart. But I lie to the pen,
not daring to describe how I ambled
along the distant ramparts of love,
barefoot, wearing a birthday suit:
the placental slime and blood.

25

I ought to remember: I was four,
she was two months and twenty days.
My sister-death is still in her grave.
I know nothing of her.
Maybe that is why in each moment of joy
an immense grief lurks,
as if I were sitting at an empty crib,
my gown wet with milk.

26

Those who are asleep in the earth
have an avian sense of the way.
Gone, they sleep with shoes on,
ready to rise and go
to the pink, dispensable,
barefooted insomniacs
who had laced up for them
the last pair of shoes.

27

Immortal: neither dead nor alive.
Immortality is fatal.
Let us embrace. Your arms are
the sleeves of a straitjacket,
a life vest to stay afloat.
Lyrical poets are cursed:
a caress is always firsthand,
a word rarely.

28

He gave me life as a gift.
What can I give in return?
My poems.
I have nothing else.
But then, are they mine?
This is the way, as a child,
I would give birthday cards
to my mother: I chose them,
and paid with my father's money.

29

The two are in love and happy.
He:
"When you are not here,
it feels as though you
had just stepped out
and are in a room next door."
She:
"When you step out
and are in a room next door,
it feels as though
you do not exist anymore."

30

Sprawling
after love:
"Look,
the ceiling is
all covered with stars!"
"And maybe
on one of them
there is life . . ."

31

Begged him: do not fall asleep!
But he did, and in the dark of the night
loneliness took hold of me, like an incubus.
Furious and rough was the onslaught
of unchaste hands: this is the way
a slave ravishes his master's wife,
a soldier rapes a schoolgirl.
—I'll tell my husband!
—You're lying.
—I'll call to him right now!
—You're raving.
You will call to no one.
You have no one to call.

32

The hush of the combat zone.
On my back, alone,
I feel your seed dying in me,
feel its fear, its wish to live on . . .
I wonder if I can carry
so many deaths inside me,
as I nurture
my own?

33

Lay down.
Embraced.
Could not decide: would I rather
sleep or sleep with him?
Afterward could not decide
what it was:
was I sleeping?
Were we?
Or the one and the other?

34

Perhaps when our bodies throb and rub
against each other, they produce a sound
inaudible to us but heard up there, in the clouds and higher,
by those who can no longer hear common sounds . . .
Or, maybe, this is how He wants to check by ear: are we still
      intact?
No cracks in mortal vessels? And to this end He bangs
men against women?

35

I do not mind being away from you.
That is not what the problem is.
You will step out to get cigarettes,
will come back, and realize I have aged.
Lord, what a pitiful,
tedious pantomime!
A click of a lighter in the dark,
one puff, and I am no longer loved.

36

To converse with the greats
by trying their blindfolds on;
to correspond with books
by rewriting them;
to edit holy edicts,
and at the midnight hour
to talk with the clock by tapping a wall
in the solitary confinement of the universe.

37

An opaque, gentle, vulnerable day,
as if it had been making love all night,
a day when the past has no bitter taste,
when the future retreats without a fight:
the seventh day after a thousand-and-one nights.

. . . In the morning Scheherazade opened the door,
and three sons stood before the King's eyes.
But to me this tale is the least credible of all.

38

Good-bye, my dear!
The bugles call.
I will kiss on the lips
the mirror in your hall.
And on the cheek. And lest I
not survive
this vicious minute, also
the handle of the closing door.

39

I have wasted such a love
that surely I am bound for hell.
With my new, proxy love
no gate in hell will let me pass.
I have ripped so many pillows,
and now, for some winters to come,
will be filling the caverns of flesh
with your body. Love, a failure all around,
a flaw in the shroud of days.
. . . will be filling the howling caverns of mind
with your heavenly flesh.

40

Sex, the sign language of the deaf and mute,
a confession of love by the mute to the blind.
Do we not know the word *love*?
Love. But the mouth is sealed,
the eyes shut. My forearm is touching
the childlike back of your head.
The blind is tender. The mute is ardent.
And the sign of accord, in unison: a cloudburst!

41

If only I knew from what tongue
your *I love you* has been translated,
if I could find the original,
consult the dictionary
to be sure the rendition is exact:
the translator is not at fault!

42

I am in love, hence free to live
by heart, to ad-lib as I caress.
A soul is light when full,
heavy when vacuous.
My soul is light. She is not afraid
to dance the agony alone,
for I was born wearing your shirt,
will come from the dead with that shirt on.

43

Multiplying in a column M by F
do we get one or two as a result?
May the body stay glued to the soul,
may the soul fear the body.
Do I ask too much? I only wish
the crucible of tenderness would melt
memories, and I would sleep, my cheek
pressed against your back, as on a motorbike . . .

44

The journey will be long.
Let us lie down, old friend.
First loves come by the dozen,
the last love is but one.
May the summer last
as a prison term
of farewell delights,
caresses on the doorstep.

45

We are rich: we have nothing to lose.
We are old: we have nowhere to rush.
We shall fluff the pillows of the past,
poke the embers of the days to come,
talk about what means the most
as the indolent daylight fades;
we shall lay to rest our undying dead:
I shall bury you, you will bury me.

46

When the very last grief
deadens all our pain,
I will follow you there
on the very next train,
not because I lack strength
to ponder the end result,
but maybe you forgot to bring
pills, a necktie, razor blades . . .

47

Should not regard, but I do:
a beggar rummaging in the dump,
two gays smooching on the bench,
a wino with blood on his shirt,
the drooping penis of an old man waiting for a trickle . . .
Should not regard. But I do.

48

Love, a Sisyphus laboring
to silence anxieties.
Let me wear your last name,
I promise not to soil it.
Not for the sake of decency,
not for any fringe benefits,
but to be more graceful and prettier
on holidays, at balls, going out.

49

Any housecoat would do,
but the seamstress cuts
the wedding gown
out of sea foam.
Come, undo my braid.
No sister's foot can fit
Cinderella's sandals
of cinders made.

50

I have brushed my teeth.
This day and I are even.

51

A Draft of a Marriage Contract

. . . if necessary, the books shall be divided as follows:
you get the odd, I get the even pages;
"the books" are understood to mean the ones we used to read
        aloud
together, when we would interrupt our reading for a kiss,
and would get back to the book after half an hour . . .

52

A weight on my back,
a light in my womb.
Stay longer in me,
take root.
When you are on top of me,
I feel triumphant and proud,
as if I were carrying you
out of a city under siege.

53

Armpits smell of linden blossom,
lilacs give a whiff of ink.
If we could only wage lovemaking
all day long without end,
love so detailed and elastic
that when nightfall came,
we would exchange each other
like prisoners of war, five times, no less!

54

Man to woman is homeland.
Woman to man is a way.
How much way have you covered!
Dear, get some rest:
here is a chest, lean your head;
here is a heart, camp out;
and we shall evenly share
the dry residue of griefs.

55

Memory keeps nothing unnecessary
    or superfluous.
How much of your past
    am I still to go through?
Taking dreams for memories,
    I stroke the sleeper's head.
A secret poll. The future
    comes in last.

56

Envy not singers and mimes,
do not ravish the ailing words.
The adjective *beloved*
embraces all other adjectives,
verbs, nouns,
pronouns . . .
Poor Logos, naked and starved,
pining in admiration!

Inseparable: the parrot and its mirror,
Narcissus and his stream.
Here, I have made duplicate keys
to Eden, had the white dress altered.
Inseparable: Robinson Crusoe and Friday,
the dots in the umlaut,
me and you, my Sunday.

58

The serenade of a car siren
under a window gone dark.
Anything but betrayal!
Let us stop ears with wax,
tie the daredevil to the woman
as to a mast . . . The sleep,
restless and moist.
The arm goes numb.

59

Writing down verses, I got
a paper cut on my palm.
The cut extended my life line
by nearly one-fourth.

60

Teeth dull, veins collapsed,
heels worn down.
We are young as long as
our parents are young.
Dry is the riverbed where milk and honey,
white and amber, had run.
In the hospital, comb your mother's hair,
clip the yellow nails.

61

Bathe me, birth me from foam,
cover me, swathe me in hugs.
Paradise is where
    nothing can ever change.
You're crying? —No, a speck in the eye.
You're crying? —No, too much reading.
Hell is where there is no way
    you can ever change.

62

You are, my dear,
a wall of stone:
to sing or howl
behind,
to bash my head on.

63

A tentative bio:
caught fireflies,
read till dawn,
fell in love with weirdos,
cried buckets of tears
for reasons unknown,
birthed two daughters
by seven men.

64

I walk the tightrope.
A kid on each arm
for balance.

65

Old age will come, will arrange books
in alphabetical order, will sort out photos and negatives.
With a head shake: "How meager the heritage of the most
      gifted."
With a shrug: "Still, they must have done their best."
Wrapping a shawl tighter: "Incredible: any man that comes
      along
can deserve the title 'darling'!"
With a toothless grin: "How lovely they look now,
the rejected photos never put into albums!"

66

A Remedy for Insomnia

Not sheep coming down the hills,
not cracks on the ceiling—
count the ones you loved,
the former tenants of dreams
who would keep you awake,
once meant the world to you,
rocked you in their arms,
those who loved you . . .
You will fall asleep, by dawn, in tears.

67

Eyes of mine,
why so sad?
Am I not cheerful?
Words of mine,
why so rough?
Am I not gentle?
Deeds of mine,
why so silly?
Am I not wise?
Friends of mine,
why so dead?
Am I not strong?

68

A cake of soap, a length of rope,
a chair to hang socks on.
Death from depression seems
a bit ridiculous.
Starless is the abyss,
dark the water's depth.
Too late for me
to have died young.

69

The sleeping are no mates for the crying,
the crying cannot judge those asleep.
How quickly you succumb to slumbers,
how blissfully, as I lie crying
next to you, hiding in the pillow
and saving for a rainy day
the lullaby to mourn the one
who had fallen asleep before I did.

70

"If you want, we can part with a smile,
or you can cry a little, if you want."
The sole profession in the world
for men only: the executioner.
Has all been properly done:
the verdict duly announced,
the scaffold set nice and comfy?
Is the ax razor sharp?

71

Self-Portrait in Profile

I
am
the one
who wakes up
on your
left.

72

At last you and I are one,
together until the end.
Penelope's cloth came in handy
for the wedding gown,
napkins, bedsheets, hankies,
with enough left for Odysseus
to make a sail.

73

A torture: writing a rough draft
of what came as a fair copy.
The milky wholeness is gone.
The waxy ripeness is here.
I take the accursed apple,
the one that deprives us of peace,
nibble on it, do not swallow,
keep the bite behind my cheek.

74

We lay down, and the pain let up.
We embraced, and the pain let go:
no more scalding regrets,
no scorching remorse
that oppressed the soul,
that weighed like a stone on the heart.
You, on top of me, heavy, immense,
and I, feeling so light.

75

A caress over the threshold
of sleep. Asleep? Half asleep?
We are ignorant of vice:
blind, entwined, content,
our bodies cling tight
to each other
without our knowledge,
ignorant of the evil.

76

Am I lovely? Of course!
Breathlessly I taste
the subtle compliment
of a handmade caress.
Chop me into tiny bits,
caress and tame my soul,
that godly swallow
you love to no end.

77

Where are we? On the sky's
seventh floor. Above seven clouds
you are sewing the soul to the flesh
with strong manly stitches
that can neither be cut nor torn.
Inseparable, as you and I:
the light vibrant flesh,
the vibrant light soul.

78

Basked in the sun,
listened to birds,
licked off raindrops,
and only in flight
the leaf saw the tree
and grasped
what it had been.

79

The matted lashes sprinkled
with pollen from Eden's tree.
Your face: the sun.
Mine: a sunflower.

80

Snapshots from Memory

I

The golden lies of May:
that nature favors me,
the sun is for me alone,
like a reading light on the plane.
Whenever I wish, I press
a button, and browse at will
through some worthless magazine
on a flight to you. And soon will land.

II

Pellets of sunburned skin,
a love bite from a gnat
next to my nipple. Eve's dress
must have been sewn for me.
An ant clambers up my arm,
a dragonfly lands on my back . . .
Stocking up summer for winter,
I know: the supply will not last.

III

A lonesome crow
croaks in the dusk.
The wind and nettles play cards;
the deck is marked.
A drinking binge next door.
An old man in the drizzling rain
carries a coat to the dump:
a woman's coat, warm, heavy cloth, hardly worn.

IV

A box for useless scrap.
A compost dump.
A puddle covered with grates
filched from the graveyard.
A bunch of frisky guys
on the way to a dance.
A scarecrow crucified
for crows to laugh at.

V

Torment: the homeland.
Happiness: a foreign land.
Patriotism: a congenital trauma.
The tears of a drunken gent
calling out to a prostitute:
"Hey, mama!"
Her grimace.
Nostalgia: craving pain.

. . . went to the movies with classmates,
came home, found his mother
hanging in the hallway.

VI

Picking a sleepy kid
off the potty at night:
the kid's limbs
a foal's,
a Christ's,
long and scrawny
in the dim light.
A *Pietà*.

VII

Another poet came into being
when I saw the life of life,
the death of death:
the child I had birthed.
That was my beginning:
blood burning the groin,
the soul soaring, the baby wailing
in the arms of a nurse.

81

I think it will be winter when he comes.
From the unbearable whiteness of the road
a dot will emerge, so black that eyes will blur,
and it will be approaching for a long, long time,
making his absence commensurate with his coming,
and for a long, long time it will remain a dot.
A speck of dust? A burning in the eye? And snow,
there will be nothing else but snow,
and for a long, long while there will be nothing,
and he will pull away the snowy curtain,
he will acquire size and three dimensions,
he will keep coming closer, closer . . .
This is the limit, he cannot get closer. But he keeps
        approaching,
now too vast to measure . . .

82

He pissed on a firefly,
but the critter took wing
and alighted on my pants,
making me jump and scream,
afraid of catching fire.
No, no harm was done.

83

At the piano: my back to the world.
At the piano: behind a high wall.
At the piano: like going down into a mine,
or on a drinking binge, taking along no one.

84

Thought's surface: word.
Word's surface: gesture.
Gesture's surface: skin.
Skin's surface: shiver.

85

Against the current of blood
passion struggles to spawn;
against the current of speech
the word breaks the oar;
against the current of thought
the sails of dreams glide;
dog-paddling like a child, I swim
against the current of tears.

86

My craft is not stringing lyres
with sunbeams, nor weaving wreaths.
Patient cutting of facets
on tears unshed, that is my craft.
Not for the sake of a gleam in the eye,
but to leave a trace behind . . .
and truly royal will be the reward:
a chance to cry the heart out.

87

Cannot look at you when you eat.
Cannot look at you when you pray,
when you extricate your leg from your pants,
when you kiss and take me.
Cannot look at you when you sleep.
Cannot look at you when you are not here.
Cannot wait until you come home again
and after a prayer sit down to eat.

88

Wrinkles around the mouth
put it in parentheses.
Wrinkles in the corners of the eyes
put them in quotation marks.
Wrinkles across the forehead
crossed out the writing on it.
Wrinkles across the neck . . .
and the bridal veil of gray hair.

89

Who will winter my immortality
with me? Who will thaw with me?
Come what may, I shall never trade
the earthly love for the subterranean.
I still have time to turn
into flowers, clay, white-eyed memory . . .
But while we are mortal, my love, to you
nothing will be denied.

90

Eternalize me just a bit:
take some snow and sculpt me in it,
with your warm and bare palm
polish me until I shine . . .

91

dropped
and falling
from such
heights
for so
long
that
maybe
I will have
enough time
to learn
flying

92

He marked the page with a match
and fell asleep in mid-kiss,
while I, a queen bee
in a disturbed hive, stay up and buzz:
half a kingdom for a honey drop,
half a lifetime for a tender word!
His face, half-turned.
Half past midnight. Half past one.

93

Spinner, do not hesitate:
while the kiss is fresh,
snip the two threads
with one swift cut.

94

On the chin, on its edge,
under the chin many a kiss . . .
The golden boat trembles
on the surface of closed eyes.
Hair, rowlocks, clavicles,
fuzzy skin, lilies, reeds . . .
Every particle of me knows
what has happened, what is bound to be.
And I proffer my face, my shoulders
to the miracle as to the wind.
Come and row. A child again,
I will sleep curled up on the stern.

95

If only I could elope
to share with you the roof and the road!
But it is easier to bend the Milky Way,
to straighten out the rainbow,
to put an end to the Chechen war,
to feed starving kids on songs.
Should I stop loving you? Wish I could!
Easier to build a house on the waves.

96

I spin my destiny myself,
in this I need no help.
They confiscated at the airport
the scissors from the Parca.
A ripe tear rolled off,
the frail shoulders shook.
But the customs fellow did not speak
a word of ancient Greek.

97

We would hide behind the house
to play the maternity ward:
would walk around with bellies stuck out,
with a shard of glass would scratch
the bellies that were feeling a chill
to make a white and pink line;
would say: it is up to you,
if the mother lives,
the baby will die,
or the other way around,
in short, it's either-or,
and no other way out.
But there is. I should have slapped
the silly midwife for her lies,
should have proudly stormed out
of that stupid maternity ward.
I would do so now. But at the time
I bathed in the bliss of shame,
shielded the belly with my hand:
let the baby live.

98

A poem is a voice-mail:
the poet has stepped out, most likely
will not be back. Please leave a message
after you hear a gunshot.

99

The voice. The handwriting. The gait.
Maybe the smell of my hair.
That's all. Go ahead,
resurrect me.

100

Only she who has breast-fed
knows how beautiful the ear is.
Only they who have been breast-fed
know the beauty of the clavicle.
Only to humans the Creator
has given the earlobe.
The humans, through clavicles
slightly resembling birds,
entwined in caresses fly
at night to the place where,
rocking the cradle of cradles,
the babe is wailing,
where on a pillow of air
the stars nestle like toys.
And some of them speak.

Acknowledgments

The author and the translator are thankful to Deborah Garrison, Derek Walcott, Valentina Polukhina and Daniel Weissbort, Alice Quinn, Yelena Demikovsky and Brian Singh, Cecile Roulet and Michael Wyler, and Svetlana Buyanina for their assistance and support in preparing this book for publication.

"One Touch in Seven Octaves" was first published in *Tin House*. "We are rich, we have nothing to lose," "If there is something to desire," "I think it will be winter when he comes," and "Let us touch each other" first appeared in *The New Yorker*. "Am I lovely? Of Course!" "Those who are asleep in the earth," "To converse with the greats," "I am in love, hence free to live," "Multiplying in a column M by F," "When the very last grief," "He marked the page with a match," and "Only she who has breast-fed" first appeared in *Poetry*. "Armpits smell of linden blossom" first appeared in *Modern Poetry in Translation 20: Contemporary Russian Women Poets*, edited by Daniel Weissbort, guest editor Valentina Polukhina (London: King's College).

A NOTE ABOUT THE AUTHOR

Vera Pavlova was born in Moscow and graduated from the Gnessin Academy of Music with a degree in history of music. She began writing poetry at the age of twenty, and is the author of seventeen collections of poetry and the librettos to five operas and four cantatas. Her poems have been translated into twenty-one languages. She is the recipient of numerous awards, including the Apollon Grigoriev Grand Prize (2001). One of the four poems by Pavlova featured in *The New Yorker* was selected by the Poetry in Motion program and was displayed in subway cars in New York City, as well as in buses in Los Angeles. She is currently one of the best-selling poets in Russia. *If There Is Something to Desire* is Pavlova's first collection in English.

A NOTE ABOUT THE TRANSLATOR

Steven Seymour is a professional interpreter and translator of Russian, Polish, and French. His Russian translations of W. H. Auden, Charles Simic, James Tate, and Billy Collins have appeared in leading Russian literary magazines, while his English translations of Vera Pavlova's poems have appeared in *Tin House* and *The New Yorker*. He has also translated poems by Zbigniew Herbert, Adam Zagajewski, and Wisława Szymborska from the Polish, as well as almost all of the French poems of Rainer Maria Rilke into English. He lives in New York City.

A NOTE ON THE TYPE

This book was set in Caledonia, a Linotype face designed by W. A. Dwiggins (1880–1956). It belongs to the family of printing types called "modern face" by printers—a term used to mark the change in style of the type letters that occurred around 1800. Caledonia borders on the general design of Scotch Roman, but it is more freely drawn than that letter.

Composed by Creative Graphics, Allentown, Pennsylvania
Printed and bound by Thomson-Shore, Dexter, Michigan
Designed by Wesley Gott